I Survived The Pain!
Poems of Life

Elizabeth Mitchell

I Survived The Pain: Poems of Life: Elizabeth Mitchell

Copyright © 2017 by Elizabeth Mitchell

All rights reserved. This book or any portion thereof may not be reproduced or used in any manner whatsoever without the express written permission of the publisher except for the use of brief quotations in a book review.

Printed in the United States of America

First Printing

ISBN 978-1-943284-12-2 (pbk.)

ISBN 978-1-943284-13-9 (ebk)

A2Z Books Publishing

1990 Young Rd

Lithonia, GA 30058

www.A2ZBooksPublishing.com

Manufactured in the United States of America

A2Z Books Publishing has allowed this work to remain exactly as the author intended, verbatim.

CONTENTS

Part 1 1
Part 2 3
    Let your past be gone 12
    Woman to Woman 13
    God's favor 16
    Look Up 17
    Life 18
    The What if of Life 19
    Encouraged 22
    A Place in Jesus's heart 23
    My God understands 24
    Decisions 25
    God's plan 26
    Lord Help me to Stand 27
    You are what I need 30
    No one but you 31
    Seasons 32
    Conclusion 33

I SURVIVED THE PAIN

PART 1

PART 1

I remember when my parents would take me to my grandparents' house to stay until they get off work and I would sit on the couch and watch Mickey Mouse. I would sit there for hours and every time I got hungry, I would go to my grandmother and say, "I am hungry again". I would eat only enough to keep me satisfied, so I could go watch more TV. Little did I know that was my first experience of survival. That same little girl is now a woman who has survived mental abuse, physical abuse, a nervous breakdown, miscarriages, financial struggle, embarrassment, abandonment, rejection, and insecurities. We all experience pain and disappointment in life, but we have to understand that God would not put more on us than we can handle. Whatever pain you can identify with or may have now, I am a witness that you can survive! **Philippians 4:13 says, "I can do all this through him who gives me strength."** Many times in life, we feel as if a situation is too much for us but let me tell you my story of Survival!

Often times, things do not go as planned, but the word of God says **"Many are the plans in a man's heart, but it is the lord's purpose that prevails. (Proverbs, 19:21, KJV)** I had many plans for myself just like you, nevertheless God had another way. At the age of nineteen, I got married to my high school sweetheart. We struggled financially because we had no guidance of how to manage our finances and keeping our marriage together as well. We had to learn so much in a short amount of time to maintain a place to stay, to budget and look forward to getting things for ourselves. Some of the problems in marriages are caused by not having enough money, but many problems were far greater than money; like the lack of communication or not loving ourselves. I have watch my mother and father build a marriage on love, respect and trust for one another and that is what I wanted for my marriage. They made it seem so easy, but when I got married, I realized that it was more than what meets the eyes. I saw marriage as a sacred, honorable, and desirable union until I experienced the pain.

As women, we know we can handle pressure most of the time better than men, but it is not that we want pressure or pain, but because we are so determined to make things work. We persevere but on the other hand, some men do not want to deal with it. Elder and I were raised in the church; our families faithfully went to church every Sunday and participated in church ministries. However, as far as he and I, we knew nothing about how to really trust God, furthermore how to keep each other encouraged. Therefore, many things started to happen in our marriage. First, lies about simple things, jealousy, and the pain of adultery that continued for a very long time. I can remember a time when we both were working at Hardees, I had been promoted to manager, and he became jealous and accused me of dating the other manger because of our meetings. One day, he made a big fuss in the restaurant, so I chose to quit in order to save my marriage. After trying so many things including prayer and counseling, we still resulted to separation. I moved back with my parents but after staying with them for weeks, I missed being on my own so Elder and I got back together. I found out later that he was cheating and the young woman had gotten pregnant. I was sitting in the Livingroom when I got the news and the feeling of defeat came over me. I felt depression like I've never felt before because the man I loved and gave my life to gave me nothing but deceit. He then moved in with his girlfriend and her family. When he left, I found myself in a sunken place where I did not want to even live anymore. My self-esteem was so low that it was hard to even get up and get dressed. Five months later, his girlfriend miscarried which made me feel bad because at an early age she experienced losing a child. Even though I was pregnant, I was learning how to endure the things I could not change. I could not change that Elder chose to leave home for someone else, but could change how I responded to the pain. **Philippians 4:12 says, "I know what it is to be in need, and I know what it is to have plenty. I have learned the secret of being content in any and every situation, whether well fed or hungry, whether living in plenty or in want."**

Later that year, I was home alone and my water broke. I only stayed approximately five to eight miles from the hospital, but I did not have a car to drive, so I had to walk. I had no way of letting anyone know of my condition and having to go to the hospital because I had no way of communication. The next day, Elder got the news and came to the hospital and he was able to make it before I delivered but hours later we found out that our baby girl didn't make it. My heart still hurts knowing that she never had the opportunity to experience the love I have for her and we will never get to do any of those mother-daughter things. I thank God even now for helping me to survive that pain. My daughter Sherri Amiricale will always be in my heart. About a year later, Elder and I decided to try to make things work concerning our marriage, but things went bad all over again. He got in trouble and was sentenced to ten years in prison. I was six months pregnant with child when he went to jail. He did not see his son until he was almost three months old. While he was in prison, I stayed faithful to him even though there were lies that surfaced, saying the child was not his child. I visited him every time he was allowed visitors, even when he was moved to different cities in North Carolina because my desire was for our marriage to work in spite of what we had gone through.

My mother-in-law and I faithfully stood by him, visiting him when no one would go. We fixed boxes of food to feed him and some of the inmates. While he was in Newton prison, he was allowed to go and visit at home for limited hours. During the time he was coming home, things began to get better for us as a family again. He began pastoring a church and we were building together spiritually, financially, and going through a process of healing. I was so elated that I wrote this poem.

Look up, put a big smile on your face, this is the dawning of a brand-new day
The battle that is going on in your mind, give it to Jesus,
He won the battle from the beginning of time.

Look up, Jesus loves you, don't hang your head down.

The truth is, he's the closest friend that will stay around.
Maybe you feel like all hope is gone, let me encourage you,
our heavenly father is on the throne. Look up; the Lord has given you
instructions on what to do. Believe the written word of God, it is true.
Just know that Jesus will never leave or forsake you.

I SURVIVED THE PAIN!

About two years went by, life had gotten much better for our family and I was with child. We were both filled with joy because we had so much that we were hoping for. In 1987, our little boy was born and the following year, my Elder was released from prison. Our family and friends all welcomed him back. Approximately one year and a half went by and I found out that he was cheating again. My heart was broken, spirit crushed and I did not know how to handle so much pain, after waiting ten years and some months for him. My mind was made up in spite of what happened I knew I must stay believing in Jesus and raise my two sons to the best of my ability. We remained in the same house but were divided. There were times where we both would be home, but we would act as if we did not exist to each other. We had no communication and our relationship affected our children. As parents, we must make sure that our children feel safe and protected in our home. Arguing builds an atmosphere of hostility. Hostility can make a child angry and they will not even realize they are angry. Furthermore, they battle with that anger for the rest of their life unless they deal with it. After realizing that living in this environment was not healthy for us nor was it changing, we decided to go our separate ways.

As I faced each day, I would say…..

Lord help me to stand and proclaim your name; in spirit and in truth. Let me not make your name ashamed in whatever I say or do. Because you are the one that died for us all, without your love, grace, and mercy, we would be lost. I am taking out time this very moment to say I love you Lord in a very special way. Lord help us stand, help me to stand.

Getting a divorce was never what I wanted for us, but we had to choose what was best for our family. Shortly afterward, he remarried. I went through the pain of being divorced; it felt like death to me. I cried many days and nights, but I made it through. I began to think why sit in misery and distress when my Lord and Savior says to me, "Rest". I had to realize that a failed marriage does not make you a failure.

The peace that lies so deeply within, Jesus fought the battle and we won. He brought me through repeatedly. We were once in captivity, but now in great liberty. My Jesus brought me through, so tell me what more can He do.

In my conclusion, I owe my life, my praises, and my service to the Lord. I made a vow to myself to love and obey God for the rest of my days. He gave me strength in my weakest moment. When I thought I was losing my mind, He was the one who sustained me. Because of Him, I survived the pain. Therefore, if you are wondering who can do the impossible and cause possibility to manifest, take this poem into thought.

Who can turn your mourning into dancing, and sorrow into joy
Your tears into laughter and cause the sun to shine thereafter
Who can make everything all right and your darkest hour to become a shining light?
Who provides for you when your resources are gone? You trusted in family and friend
but then you were left alone
Who comes in a still voice and give you peace, knowing I can rest assured that I am
loved when I go to sleep
When your heart has been broken, remember your life is not a token
Who can make you feel loved when you are going through a lonely storm

I SURVIVED THE PAIN!

Who can give you an undignified praise and sweet savor worship from the heart
Who can make your dreams come true, even when the enemy says you are washed up and through
Who Can, The Lord God can
He is strong and mighty and never leaves his throne
Our Lord and savior Jesus Christ will never leave us alone

LETTER FROM THE AUTHOR

I hope you were encouraged by my testimony "I survived the pain". God has it on my heart to reach people like myself who need to know that God can bring you through anything. You cannot only survive the pain, but overcome it and live in God's abundance. I saw the hand of God move many times throughout my life, even through the storms. Remember to stay focused on God and not focused on the storm. Many times, we make decisions based on what we see when God is only saying trust me. I hope that part two of the book encourages you to live the abundant life that God planned before you! You were so worth it that He gave his only son for you! Jeremiah 29:11

Minister, Elizabeth Mitchell

I SURVIVED THE PAIN

PART 2

ELIZABETH MITCHELL

LET YOUR PAST BE GONE

When your past tries to make a way to come in your present, don't think twice to wonder should I, let it stay absent

The Lord gives us new mercies each and every day, don't let the things of your past find you wanting them to stay.

Let the misery of your past GO!

Let your past be gone because with Jesus we are never alone

Occupy your time doing the things that are pleasing to God

Put your faith and trust in Him and thank the Lord for a brand-new start.

You may feel as though you have lost a lot, but let your past be gone

Now, you really know the truth from your heart

Keep the promises of God fresh in your mind, and let go of all negative thoughts and people and leave them behind

I have let my past go and I have new life from both outside and within

Life is so much sweeter, my sisters and brothers. I never want to go back to my past again. I challenge you this day to let your past stay away.

WOMAN TO WOMAN

Woman to Woman, come now let us reason together with a sincere heart and mind

Let the love of God manifest woman to woman, this is our time

When we all come together, touching and agreeing on the same thing. Satan is defeated no matter what he brings

Woman to woman, we must make a stand, and let's go about God's business, impacting the lost, "Jesus" paved the way with his life he paid the cost

Some of us may have been in a place when we thought all hope was gone

But by the grace and mercy of God, we came back strong

These words I must leave with you, depend totally on "Jesus Christ" because he is our answer and He will see us through

ELIZABETH MITCHELL

NOTES

NOTES

ELIZABETH MITCHELL

GOD'S FAVOR

God's favor will enable you to go places that you thought would never be an open door

When Gods favor is in and on your life, you will realize He is good and Oh so kind

Now, give God praise like you are losing your mind

When God's favor is working in your life, it is with power and demonstration and without reservation.

It has been said that favor isn't fair remember, from the pit to a wealthy place

God did it, and He really does care

God is so awesome in all His ways, trust in Him totally and be obedient my sisters and my brothers

You will see better days

This is God's favor

LOOK UP

Look up, put a big smile on your face

This is a dawning of a brand-new day

The battle that is going on in your mind

Give it to Jesus, he has already won the battle from the beginning of time

Look up, and live, enjoy life and tell peace be still!

Look up, Jesus loves you, don't hang your head down

The truth is He's the closest friend around

Maybe you feel like all hope is gone,

Let me encourage you, our heavenly father is on the throne

Look up, the Lord has given instructions on what to do

Just believe the written words He has given to you

Know that God is faithful and He is true, Look up

ELIZABETH MITCHELL

LIFE

Whom shall I fear? The Lord is with me far and near

My life and my soul depends on the Lord

Without Him, Ohhh what a void

My strength totally comes from above

Jesus is always showering us with His unconditional love

I thank God for sending his son "Jesus" to die for us all

Sinners you must come to Jesus, He'll bring you out

I know this without a doubt

Life without the Lord is surely a waste of time

The years that have gone by cannot be regained

Don't waste your life away, trust God and thank Him in advance for brighter days

Choose a life of prosperity

Pray, obey and above all, believe

Life can be wonderful, just don't be deceived

THE WHAT IF OF LIFE

What if I stop coming and just be, lives could be changed just by hearing my testimony

What if I speak wisdom and power over everything my hands touch, does that mean I am vessel?

God is using to show His marvelous work though

What if you are stuck in the past, Arise! Get your mind sobered, only what we do for God will last

What if I did less than my best, I would be defeating myself

What if someone you love walked away?

How would you handle that? Let them go and don't beg them to stay

What if prayers you prayed came to past

Would you show your gratitude, and good attitude or would you reply ungratefully "at last"?

What if we let God have the final say, He will fix everything

He endured the nails because everything He does, He does well

What if you walk into the room, and the atmosphere change, don't get it twisted, it is the anointing that cause you to never be the same

NOTES

NOTES

ELIZABETH MITCHELL

ENCOURAGED

When no one seems to really care
I know Jesus said "I will never leave you, I will be right there"
"I am encouraged"
In life, things do not always go as planned, just don't make excuses or blame the other man
Be real about it all, keep your head up, and remember God won't let you fall
"I am encouraged"
When your back is against the wall and you can't see a way out
Hoping and praying for a better day
God always steps in and creates a way
"I am encouraged"
Just knowing that God really loves me
That makes me smile and hold my head up
Knowing your self-worth is far more than you can see
"I am encouraged"
What God has for me is for me, it is for me
"I am encouraged"
Today, I would like to encourage you in everyway
Be thankful and grateful right where you are and stay humble while reaching for the stars
Stay in right alignment and obey
God's word, dismiss all negative you have heard
Don't be focused on how and stressing on when, because with God on our side, we shall win. "I am encouraged"

A PLACE IN JESUS'S HEART

Kings kids have a place in Jesus's heart

We must stand together so that they will have a better start

A brighter future for them we see

Just imagine what they can grow and be

Let us come together with the Love of God

that He will lead us all the way

with the grace and mercy of His love

The Kings kid will never go astray

ELIZABETH MITCHELL

MY GOD UNDERSTANDS

Many times I haven't done all that was right

My God understands my pains, and sleepless nights

So glad God is not like man, He understands

Sometimes, I don't know what to do, God way is always right

He's there to see me safely through, oh how my God understands

Aren't you glad to know that in spite of our own demands, God still understands?

So please, don't judge your fellow man because even for them, God still understands

I love Him so, because He will never leave my side

I'm always thanking Him for being my guide

Thanking Him for loving me from my head to my feet

Without His love where would I be?

My God understands

DECISIONS

We must make decisions everyday

Sometimes, they are good and some we wonder if we should

There are so many things that goes through our minds

But in spite of those thoughts, we must make decisions all the time

Every choice isn't going to be so pleasant

The matter could very well be pressing you down

Be very sure you seek the Lord while He may be found

Let no one control your mind, stand, and stand tall

Or you won't have a mind at all

2016 has been titled "Destiny Decision"

So, let our focus be on the things of God

As He make clear our vision

The decisions we make can very well determine our lifelong dream

It is imperative to think it out, most definitely pray, and say what you mean

Decisions, Decisions

ELIZABETH MITCHELL

GOD'S PLAN

Many are the plans in a man's heart, but it is the Lord's purpose that will prevail

Many have made many plans and we can, but the conclusion is in God's hand

He knows what is best even before we can think what is next

God has a much better plan for our lives

Just trust in Him and His plan and we shall have super natural success and sweat-less victory as we wait to arrive

No matter what you may face along the way

Follow God's plan and enjoy the joy, love and peace

God is giving you a brand new day and the old has passed away

LORD HELP ME TO STAND

Lord Help me to stand and proclaim your name in spirit and in truth

Let me not shame your name in whatever I say or do

Because you are the one who died for us all

Without your love, grace and mercy, we all will be lost

Even though I've made many mistakes

I love you Lord in a very special way

Standing in your presence makes my life so much easier

My mind, my emotions, every part of me moving with the glory that surrounds me

Lord thank you for helping me to stand

I know for sure, you are the only one with all of the power and I know that you are well able

Lord you are my strength, help me to keep standing

NOTES

NOTES

ELIZABETH MITCHELL

YOU ARE WHAT I NEED

Jesus you are all I need, you are the air I breathe

I feel awakened by your love with every breathe I take

Jesus, you are all I need, I really need you every day and in every way

Knowing that all things are possible, there is nothing I can't do

You are what I need when I experience pain

I've come to realize that it all works out for my gain

Jesus you are what I need, I lift my hands surrendering my life, my will, and my ways to you

You are what I need and not trusting you is long overdue

If we don't have you dreams couldn't come true

Even in the darkest moments, you give me favor to get through

You are the reason I keep a smile on my face

I will keep you in my heart and finish this race

You are what I need

NO ONE BUT YOU

Lord there is nothing anyone can do like you

Dreams may die, or dreams may come true

But whatever the outcome may be, there is no one like you

We can think and we can dream, but no one but you can make a dream come true

Feeling sad, mind confused, what do I say, just wondering what am I supposed to do

I do remember that our help comes from no one but you

You are the creator

No one will ever be greater

My heart beats because of your unconditional love

My heavenly father you are the one who send miracles from above

ELIZABETH MITCHELL

SEASONS

Season are very important to man

Just remember the King's heart is in the Lord's hands

Don't miss your season trying to do things on your own

Because the result will turn out wrong

Wait on the Lord's timing and don't miss your season

If you do, then what you say or do will it be a legitimate reason?

There is a time and season for all things

We should live in hope and have great expectation for all good things that it brings

This is my season and I am thanking and praising God for all the right reasons

CONCLUSION

Pain and suffering has many forms. The pain and anguish can tempt a person to turn back, to surrender or to give up. However, I held onto hope and faith knowing that the Lord would bring me out of bondage. And in spite of our circumstances we should believe. Trials will come to refine your faith, but when they come, remain faithful to God. No matter what pain or trial we face in this life, we know it is not our final experience. One day we will live with Christ forever. All of the pain and shame and the many things I survived was working together for my good. Just do not give up. **Galatians.6:9 "And let us not grow weary while doing good, for in due season we shall reap if we do not lose heart."** *I thank God I* didn't die in my wilderness. I held onto God's promises. I reminded myself he said he would never leave me nor forsake me. I am yet holding to it even now in this moment. God's grace is sufficient and his strength is made perfect in my weakness.

"But he was wounded for our transgressions, he was bruised for our iniquities: the chastisement of our peace was upon him; and with his stripes we are healed." Isaiah 53:5

Thanks
Minister, Elizabeth Mitchell

Today, I encourage you take authority over your life and know you are valuable not only to yourself, but to God. You went through what you experienced so that you can help someone else, so do not take your testimony for granted. Go tell someone about the goodness of the Lord because you have SURVIVED!

Contact Info

Elizabethmitchell@gmail.com
Facebook/Eliz Mitchell

Order online at amazon.com and all other online distributors

Interested in Writing and or Publishing a BOOK???

Visit: www.A2ZBooksPublishing.com

I SURVIVED THE PAIN!

www.ingramcontent.com/pod-product-compliance
Lightning Source LLC
Chambersburg PA
CBHW021200080526
44588CB00008B/433